JOURNALS FOR EVERYONE

Journals For Everyone
ISBN 10- 198664510X
ISBN 13 - 978-1986645102

44009599R00056

Made in the USA
Middletown, DE
01 May 2019